WORLD ON A GLASS PLATE

Early Anthropological Photographs
from the Pitt Rivers Museum, Oxford

Elizabeth Edwards
Lynne Williamson

Pitt Rivers Museum
University of Oxford

ISBN 0 902793 15 2
Copyright © 1981 Pitt Rivers Museum

Published by Pitt Rivers Museum Publications Department, Oxford
Set in Monophoto Baskerville
Printed and bound in Great Britain by Balding + Mansell, Wisbech, Cambs.

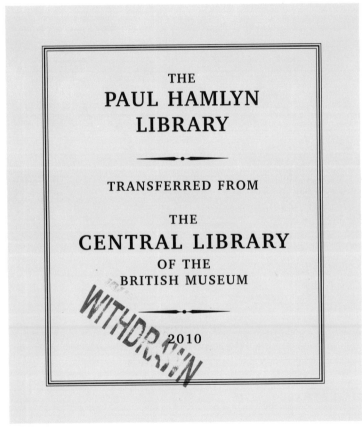
Front cover:
NEW GUINEA. c. 1884
Photographer: Rev. W. G. Lawes. Donor: E. B. Tylor

Lakatoi under full sail. Every year these multi-hulled canoes sail from Port Moresby to the Gulf of Papua and back carrying a large cargo of pots which is traded for sago. The journey is accompanied by much ritual and celebration both on land and on board.

CONTENTS

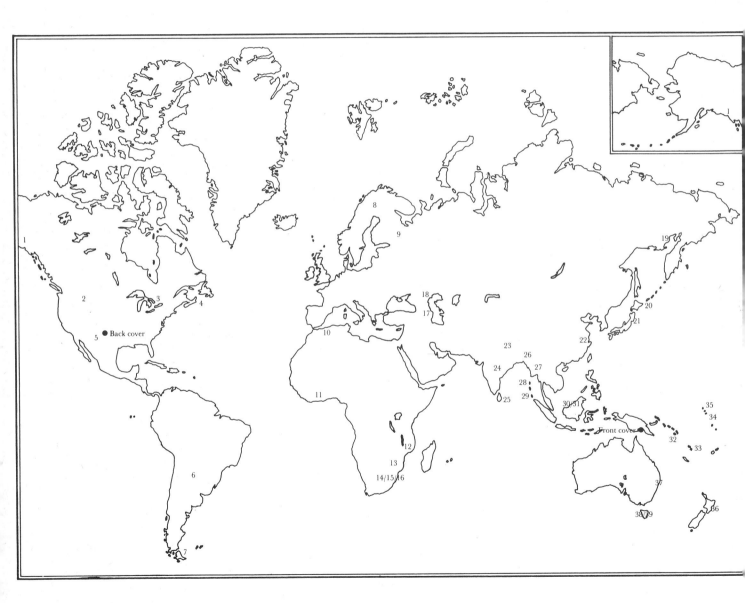

FOREWORD

'Photos I find are so important an adjunct to a museum that I try to beg all I can for a series I am making for the Museum.' This was written in 1898 by Henry Balfour, the first Curator of the Pitt Rivers Museum, to Baldwin Spencer, a leading specialist on Australian aboriginal culture. Balfour's collection of photographs, which he built up over fifty years, forms the core of the Museum's photographic archive. He was ahead of his time in realising the value of such documentation to elucidate and complement collections of material culture. Sailors and travellers had been bringing back objects from other cultures for many centuries but only in the nineteenth century were these collections organised, studied on a scientific basis and made available to a wider public through museums.

Interest in anthropology as we know it also developed apace in the nineteenth century, inspired by a wider knowledge of the world in general and to some extent by Charles Darwin's theories of evolution. Scholars began to examine the living races of mankind to look for an evolutionary pattern in societies from 'stone age' man to 'civilised' man. However, as more work was done and anthropologists spent at least short periods living among the communities they studied, it became clear that 'primitive' cultures were, in fact, very intricate, with complex systems of social organisation and religious beliefs and a technology to meet their specific needs.

The collection of accurate information became of paramount importance in order to understand more fully all the interrelated aspects of the cultures studied. In 1874 the British Association for the Advancement of Science published a small book entitled *Notes and Queries on Anthropology* for the detailed guidance of those collecting data in the field, and in it acknowledged the advantages of photography in such ethnographic research. The value of still photographs lies in their preservation of moments in time. They can be referred to again and again for information, perhaps now lost, about the details of a particular group of people and their culture, showing the way in which objects were made and used, the environment of the people who made them, the relationships between the sexes and age groups, their use of space. All these data are vital if the objects themselves, now in museum collections, are fully to be comprehended.

Many of the earliest photographs were full-face and profile portraits or anatomical studies of different 'races', reflecting an interest in physical anthropology. The photographs often complemented meticulous measurements of man's physical make-up, the proportions of the skull or length of limb, for instance; for such data were used to help determine racial characteristics.

Until the second half of the 1870's photographs of ritual activities, daily life and technological processes actually taken in the field were fairly unusual. There were good technical reasons for this. From about 1852 until well into the 1870's, 'wet plate' photography was the standard process. By this method a glass plate was dipped in collodion (a light-sensitive chemical solution), placed in the camera while still wet, exposed for a few seconds and developed immediately, all before the collodion had dried. This process required a large amount of equipment – a heavy camera, glass plates, chemicals, storage tanks for clean water, developing dishes and a portable dark room tent – all of which had to be carried on expeditions. The adverse effects of extremes of temperature and humidity caused additional problems.

In the early 1870's the 'dry plate' was introduced and was in common use by the 1880's. This process had considerable advantages; the glass plates were covered with a dry light-sensitive emulsion which needed no preparation and did not have to be developed immediately if stored correctly. Many interesting field photographs date from this period; for example plates 9 and 30.

The end of the nineteenth century saw the introduction of cellulose film, the high speed of which meant that quick snapshots could be taken using less bulky equipment. Many anthropologists still preferred glass plates despite their disadvantages, since early film tended to deteriorate in tropical climates. The third edition of *Notes and Queries*, 1899, advised that cameras for use in the tropics should be 'made of well-seasoned wood and brass bound' to prevent damage. It also recommended taking spare parts for rubber fittings as the originals were likely to perish quickly.

Some caution is necessary when using certain types of photograph for research, particularly, although not always, the studio portraits. The photographer may have misinterpreted cultural details: he may have arranged certain elements for 'artistic effect' or for ethnocentric reasons, possibly for the demands of a developing tourist trade. Plates 21 and 37 provide examples of scenes and portraits which imply attitudes and uses of objects which are now known to be incorrect: the Japanese girl would not be allowed out for a ride on her own without a chaperone; the aborigine Louis wears a wallaby skin loincloth only as a concession to the modesty of the viewer – his normal attire would be more scanty. Occasionally the work of a particular photographer can be recognised by the 'props' used in his studio.

Finally, a further consideration must be the effect on the subjects of being photographed. The 1951 edition of *Notes and Queries* warned on page 354:
'. . . if the camera is one with which focusing is done on a ground-glass screen with the aid of a dark cloth, great care must be exercised in using it among people unaccustomed to photography. The manipulations under the dark cloth may suggest black magic, with disastrous results, and if, as will certainly happen, onlookers wish to look in the focusing screen, they will probably be frightened by seeing people and objects upside down.'
This can be seen here in plate 16.

Others did not take the process so seriously; C. F. Wood reported in *A Yachting Cruise in the South Seas*, 1873, page 11:
'. . . I was particularly anxious to get some portraits of the natives.

We did not, however, meet with much success, for, strange to say, these people, so civilized and so keen and sensible in any matter of trading, could not be persuaded to look upon being photographed in anything but a ludicrous light. For did one of them after much persuasion consent to sit, then a crowd would gather round, especially the women, and by tittering and laughing and making remarks, make the intending subject such an object of ridicule that he would fairly take to his heels. So that when poor Mr. Smith, who had been perspiring in the tent preparing a plate, reappeared upon the scene, he would be greeted with a silly shout of laughter, and have to begin his solicitations again for a fresh subject. Some of the chiefs at last submitted to be taken, but even then the people's natural respect for their rulers scarcely prevented them from cracking jokes at their expense. I found it very difficult to keep my temper; in fact, some people might say I did not succeed: and towards evening I returned to the vessel thoroughly fagged out.'

*   *   *

Throughout the descriptive captions a form of narrative in the 'ethnographic present tense' has been used. This has been adopted to emphasise the immediacy of the still photograph which tells a story unchanged in the terms of the photograph itself, even though most of the cultures shown in this book have now either disappeared or have changed greatly through the expansion and influence of the developed world.

CANADA, NORTHWEST COAST. c. 1865–1870
Photographer: Dammann Studio. Purchased 1901

A group of medicine men (shamans). The Northwest Coast is a rich land of rivers, forests and mountains. Indian tribes such as the Haida and Tsimshian exploit the sea and salmon streams for their main foods. They use wood for their utensils, houses and elaborate carvings, including totem poles.

Mountain goats provide the stiff hair which is woven into cloaks known as 'Chilkat blankets' because they are usually made by Chilkat Tlingit women. Copper and vegetable dyes produce blue, yellow and black patterns on a natural wool background. The designs represent the animal forms of the supernatural beings who are the ancestors of the person wearing the cloak.

The shaman is an important member of these tribes, since he performs dances and ceremonies which are believed to invoke the good graces of guardian spirits. Their full regalia, seen here, includes dance shirts, aprons and leggings of the same woven technique as the cloaks, mounted on buckskin with a fringe of puffin beaks. The head-dresses are carved wooden animal masks with abalone shell inlay, sea lion whiskers as plumes, and ermine skin tassels. They carry carved wooden dance rattles.

2

NORTH AMERICA, GREAT PLAINS, Absaroka (Crow) tribe. c. 1870's
Photographer: Jackson? Donor: E. B. Tylor

The Absaroka, like other Plains Indians, were wandering hunter-gatherers. During the eighteenth and early nineteenth centuries their culture, based on the buffalo (bison) hunt, flourished. The buffalo provided for most needs: meat, skin for *tipi* covers, clothing, bags and pouches, dried dung for fuel. This photograph, taken in the 1870's, marks the demise of Plains culture, as Europeans and white Americans moved westwards in search of land and the buffalo, exploiting the skins for commercial leather and the bones for fertiliser. The Absaroka were restricted to one reservation in Montana in 1875.

Early travellers often remarked on the special dignity and beauty of the Absaroka. This brave personifies power in battle – his successes can be measured by the scalp locks hanging from his bead neck ornament. His long hair is braided on the sides and left hanging down the back, the greased forelock combed straight up with a buffalo tongue or porcupine tail. Women make exquisite tanned-skin dresses, shirts and leggings, often embroidered like this with dyed porcupine quills. The round white discs hanging from his necklace are polished buffalo shoulder blades.

CANADA, ONTARIO. 14th September 1871
Photographer: Foster. Donor: E. B. Tylor

Six of the fifty chiefs of the Six Nations of the Iroquois, 'People of the Longhouse'. This confederacy comprises the following tribes: the Seneca, Cayuga, Onondaga, Oneida, Mohawk and Tuscarora. They inhabited the strategically important trading region along Lake Ontario and the St. Lawrence River. Because most of the tribes sided with the British during the American Revolution, they were moved from New York State to land along the Grand River in Ontario.

The governing council of the Confederacy, founded by Hiawatha and Deganawidah, is composed of chiefs selected by senior women of the tribal clans. The photograph shows from left to right: Hahriron, 'He who scatters', Onondaga fire-keeper; George Johnson, 'Double life', Mohawk government interpreter; Skanawidah, 'Beyond the swamp', Onondaga wampum-keeper; John Smoke Johnson, 'Disappearing mist', Mohawk council speaker; Isaac Hill, 'the voice suspended', Onondaga fire-keeper; Seneca Johnson, 'Entangled hair', of the Snipe Clan of the Seneca.

They hold the tribal wampum records, made from purple and white shell beads strung in patterns whose symbols illustrate the treaties and agreements between tribes and with Whites. The gift of a wampum string confirms an agreement and holds immense value for the Indians.

CANADA, NOVA SCOTIA, MicMac tribe. May 1873
Photographer: 'Challenger' Expedition. Donor: H. Balfour

The MicMac live in a densely forested region full of lakes and rivers. They hunt seal, beaver, otter, caribou, porcupine and moose in winter. Spring and summer for them mean catching fish and gathering roots, nuts and berries. Hunting is of prime importance for MicMac survival; a boy does not fully become a man until he kills his first big game. This man hunts with the traditional bow of fir wood with deer or moose sinew string. Wooden arrows have flaked flint points and are fletched with woodpecker feathers.

Women set up the tents, making a frame of poles and branches bound with cedar bark fibre, which is covered with overlapping strips of matted grass and birch bark stitched together with spruce root. A skin flap covers the opening which faces south. The central hearth keeps the tent warm; pine boughs, moose skins and beaver pelts cover the floor.

The costume here is typical nineteenth-century dress, although the man wears a chief's coat of blue trade cloth with embroidery of dyed porcupine quill, moosehair or glass beads, which would be reserved for special occasions.

U.S.A., NEW MEXICO, Zuni Pueblo. 1879
Photographer: J. Hillers. Donor: E. B. Tylor

The Zuni inhabit the desert region around the Upper Rio Grande in New Mexico. They raise maize, beans, squash and cotton, and tend sheep and cattle. The precarious environmental conditions may partly account for the complex religious and ceremonial elements which are so important to the Zuni. Every boy joins one of the ceremonial fraternities or medicine societies. They enact rituals which they hope will ensure rainfall, good harvests and healthy livestock. People deck themselves in paint, eagle feathers, blankets, silver and turquoise jewellery, impersonating their ancestors and supernatural beings. Offering sticks covered with the tail feathers and down of eagles are 'planted' in the ground to promote fertility.

The Zuni keep eagles in mud cages. The feathers are considered sacred because, in Zuni mythology, the eagle flies near the zenith of the world. Medicine men can draw out sickness with the aid of an eagle feather. During the plucking ceremony the tame bird is brought to a ritual house (*kiva*) and while being held with its head facing west is plucked by a priest. Then he forces a mixture of maize and white clay down its throat to induce a lush growth of white down and long feathers.

SOUTH AMERICA, PARAGUAYAN CHACO, Lengua tribe. c. 1900
Photographer and donor: Andrew Pride, South American Missionary Society, 1903

These girls are dressed for the ritual dance of the *Yanmama* feast celebrating their coming-of-age. They wear the usual woman's costume of an untanned deerskin skirt, with ceremonial waistbands and headbands of plumes from the three-toed ostrich (rhea). Their other adornments consist of shell and teeth necklaces and rhea feather anklets which are believed to protect against snakebite. The puberty ritual is marked by a dance which dramatises the supernatural dangers which the Indians fear. The girls dance in a circle, striking the ground with these long canes, causing the deer hooves at the top to rattle. Boys with masks, representing evil spirits, pretend to threaten the girls, who drive them off.

In the background stands a Chaco house constructed of timbers with a grass roof. Indians of this arid region mainly subsist by hunting rhea, deer and wild pigs (peccary), and gathering wild fruits. They must move frequently to find new sources of food.

SOUTH AMERICA, TIERRA DEL FUEGO, Ona tribe. 1900–1902
Photographer: Lucas Bridges

Tierra del Fuego (Land of Fire) lies at the southernmost tip of South America. The terrain is rough – generally mountainous and barren, or covered with dense swampy forests. The climate is cold, damp and windy. The Ona live in the inland mountains, hunting birds, fish, foxes and especially guanaco (a form of llama) and collecting berries, fungus and grasses. Their simple culture has few tools, technological processes or ceremonies. Small family groups like this one need to move constantly in search of food. The guanaco provides the staple food, skin cloaks and moccasins, and the only shelter – a rough windbreak of skins and branches. Men hunt with bows made from beechwood, and arrows of holly or berry wood with points skilfully flaked from stone or glass found on the shore.

   We know that Halah, the man on the right, engaged in a wrestling bout in order to settle a serious vendetta relatively peacefully. Men wrestle naked, their bodies smeared with red paint, and they observe strict rules such as 'no biting'. According to Lucas Bridges, Halah lost.

SWEDISH LAPLAND, KARESUANDO. c. 1890's
Photographer: Unknown. Donor: H. Balfour, 1898

A group of Lapps by their turf house. Lapp economy depends on the reindeer which thrive in the arctic areas of Scandinavia and this demands a semi-nomadic existence for the people. In winter they travel with the herds into the forest areas using skis, reindeer sleds and, increasingly, snowmobiles. During the spring and summer months the Lapps follow their reindeer into the mountains, where the herds graze on lichen and breed. The summer house has a wooden frame from which hangs the central cooking pot. Over the frame lies a layer of birch bark, then thick turf. There is a top opening for smoke and a door.

The Lapps are famous for their colourful embroidered costumes, but those are worn only for special occasions. Women weave their ribbon decorations on small bone 'looms' and tan reindeer skins by soaking them in birch bark water. The people here wear summer clothes: men in reindeer-skin belted tunics, tight leggings and pointed moccasins; women in wool skirts, skin jackets and brightly patterned shawls. The domed wool caps with red pompoms are characteristic of the region.

FINLAND/U.S.S.R., EAST KARELIA. 1894
Photographer: I. K. Inha. Donor: Dr. V. Hern, 1899

Karelia is a vast region of sub-arctic forests, lakes and plains astride the border between Finland and the U.S.S.R. Until the beginning of this century the economy was based on animal husbandry, fishing and shifting cultivation, supplemented by fur trading and reindeer herding.

The East Karelians speak their own distinct dialect of Finnish. It is a very rich and expressive language with a powerful tradition of oral poetry and folk tale. In this photograph two men, wearing traditional felt coats, are reciting verses to one another, swaying back and forth as they chant. This was one of the ways in which the wealth of traditional ballads, poems, histories, epics and genealogies has been passed down the generations. In the early nineteenth century the Finnish scholar, Elias Lönnrot, travelled widely in Karelia collecting over 20,000 of these verses around the villages and farms. In 1835 he published a compilation of many of them – the *Kalevala* (Land of the Heroes) which has become the national epic of Finland.

10 AFRICA

ALGERIA, ORAN PROVINCE. c. 1890
Photographer: Unknown. Purchased in Algiers by H. Balfour

This Arab woman holding her child probably lives in one of the oasis towns dotting the caravan routes of North Africa. Her veil suggests that she is not Berber or Tuareg, since women of those groups go unveiled, but her particular tribe cannot be determined. She wears the common desert costume of a simple grey, white or blue *djellaba* or long cotton dress, with a white cotton cloak (*haik*) thrown over the head and shoulders to cover the face. Muslim women usually veil their faces in the presence of strangers and often in front of men of their own family as a sign of modesty. The dark leather pouch around the child's neck carries a written verse from the Koran as a charm against sickness.

GHANA. The Akan. c. 1900
Photographer: F. W. Ensor? Purchased: Mrs Ensor, 1935

A senior chief with his entourage. The quality of his dress and the large state umbrella indicate his importance. The umbrella, probably made of silk and velvet represents 'the Covering of the Nation' and is symbolic of the power of the chief. It is always held over his head by official umbrella carriers, except when protocol demands that he must step from beneath it to greet more important chiefs such as the King of Asante.

The Chief is dressed in very fine cloth which appears to be painted with Islamic inscriptions and wears sandals decorated with gold discs. The entourage are also wearing fine cloths which demonstrate a number of other decorative textile techniques found in West Africa, for example tie-dyed, wax-resist dyed and woven patterns.

There are some puzzling features in this photograph such as the gold discs worn round the women's necks (these discs are usually worn by men) and the Chief's unusual head-dress. Consequently it is difficult to identify the location exactly.

MOZAMBIQUE, Shangaan. c. 1900
Photographer: G. A. Turner? Donor: G. A. Turner, 1911

The Shangaan are a Bantu-speaking people. They live in settled villages with a mixed economy of livestock herding, particularly cattle, and crop production.

This photograph, although probably posed, shows an interesting range of Shangaan drums. The large drum (*ngoma*) is carved from a single block of wood with a membrane pegged tightly over it. To the left is a smaller version of the *ngoma*. The remaining three drums are of the *ndzumba* type. They are tall and slightly conical in shape; again a single membrane is pegged over a wooden body. Both types are beaten with a stick; the player's other hand sometimes rests on the drum-head to alter the note. The drums have specific uses, sometimes giving their name to occasions; for example, the *ngoma* drum is used for 'beer drinks' (*ngoma*).

In the background are typical Shangaan huts. The impressive roofs are made upside-down on the ground. When the framework is complete it is lifted into place by the village men who are rewarded with beer. The roofs are thatched with bundles of long grass.

SOUTH AFRICA, Zulu or Matabele. c. 1865–70
Photographer: Dammann Studio. Purchased 1901

This photograph poses a problem. Although the records describe it as Matabele, the style of the dress, weapons and hut is Zulu. The exact date of the photograph is, as yet, unknown but crucial. The period 1860–1880 saw rapid change. In the first half of the nineteenth century Zulu and Matebele styles were almost indistinguishable from one another. However by c. 1880 significant differences had developed, owing in part to the impossibility of obtaining certain materials north of the Limpopo river, for example, the monkey tails worn in the kilt of the central figure.

These men are in full warrior dress of skins and feathers. The shields are made of ox-hide, decorated at the top with a wild-cat's tail. The hide is specially prepared to harden it. The craftsmen who make such shields, cutting the hide freehand, are highly regarded. Spears are the main weapon. They are carried in bundles behind the shield in the left hand, leaving the right hand free for stabbing. A bundle of three spears is just discernible tucked behind the shield on the centre right. The elaborate head-dress is made of ostrich feathers and, if Zulu, blue crane, set into rush cord.

SOUTH AFRICA, NATAL, Zulu. 1896
Left (14): Photographer: Unknown. Purchased from the Trappist Mission, Mariannhill
Right (15): Photographer: J. E. M. Donor: H. Balfour

The Zulu of Natal are a proud people with an intricate social structure and a history of warfare against neighbouring tribes and the British, who finally defeated them in 1879. They measure wealth by their cattle herds, practise some agriculture – mainly millet, maize, pumpkins, potatoes – and live in villages of large families governed by a head man.

In Zulu society a person's role or status and age can be told from his or her dress. Infants go naked, but older children adopt a string waistband which becomes wider with age, forming an apron. Young girls may wear beaded aprons or white cloths over their shoulders; boys may wear an untanned skin buttock covering. Only young girls may wear white garments, since the Zulu see white as a symbol of purity. Adolescent girls show they are ready for courting by adopting much ornamentation: elaborately beaded skirts, bead necklaces and anklets, copper or brass armlets. Boys of this age wear loincloths of skin strips, called *umutsha*. Hairdressing is important for all; girls favour ringlets wound with fibre and greased, hanging over the forehead, while courting men put beads and flowers into their hair. Everyone has pierced ears.

Marriage changes a person's position, and clothing reflects this. Women cover themselves with a long untanned cowhide tunic (*isiDiya*) or a cloth fastened over the shoulder until the birth of the first child and thereafter during every pregnancy. The children are wrapped in these cloths slung over the mother's back. Married women arrange their hair into high pointed topknots; the woman sitting on the ground in the centre of plate 16 shows this. Also in this plate, married men with their animal-tail loincloths, thick bead necklaces and waxed leaf-fibre headrings can be seen. The headring is a sign of manhood and tearing it off gives a grave insult.

Plates 14 and 15 show newly married women. The bead and perfumed-wood necklaces, plus the 'Jubilee Whisky, Glasgow' medallion, mark the woman in the portrait as the wife of a head man or chief. The two women are touching hands and clicking their fingers in a hand game. A large beer-pot sits beside them; perhaps they are playing at a feast, where beer always provides a popular refreshment.

Plate 16 shows an amusing village scene. Against the background of the Zulu beehive grass huts, a Trappist monk from the mission near Durban instructs the warriors as they pose for one of their fellows acting as cameraman. Everyone seems unconcerned except the subjects, who look terrified.

SOUTH AFRICA, NATAL, Zulu. 1896
Photographer: unknown
Purchased from the Trappist Mission, Mariannhill

U.S.S.R., GEORGIA, Khevsur. c. 1865–70
Photographer: Dammann Studio. Purchased 1901

The Khevsurs live in scattered groups in the remote mountainous region of the east Caucasus practising a mixed economy of animal husbandry and crop production. Their name means 'People of the Valleys'. Although they speak a dialect of Georgian, the Khevsurs are no longer intelligible to the Georgians themselves. The region has had an unsettled history and after centuries of fighting with the Persians, Turks and Russians it was finally annexed to Russia in 1878. Fighting and vendetta play a prominent part in Khevsur culture. The men in this photograph are wearing chain-mail suits, the design of which dates back to the Middle Ages. They are carrying muskets, shields of wood and metal and long curved swords.

Although nominally Christian, Khevsur religion is a mixture of traditional beliefs, such as tree and earth spirits, Christianity and Islam – an amalgam of centuries of different influences.

U.S.S.R., KALMYTSKAYA, Nogai tribe. c. 1865–1870
Photographer: Dammann Studio. Purchased 1901

The Nogai are a nomadic people from the steppes west of the Caspian Sea. Although of Tartar origin they have been influenced and sometimes assimilated by other nomadic groups, particularly the Kalmuck Mongols who moved into the traditional Nogai grazing lands in the seventeenth century.

This photograph shows a group of Nogai outside their tent (*yurt*) which is typical of the region. A framework of expandable lattice wall sections, bound with a tension band, carries straight willow roof poles that rise to a circular crown. The size of a *yurt* is usually described by the number of wall sections used. The whole structure is covered with layers of felt, up to eight in winter. The outer layer is waterproofed with oil. Here the top of the *yurt* is open for ventilation, however the flap can be pulled across when necessary.

When the group move on to fresh grazing for their herds of horses, sheep and cattle the *yurt* is dismantled. It can be carried by two pack animals, one for the framework, the other for the felt covering. Like other nomadic peoples the Nogai's possessions are designed for maximum ease of transport and economy of space.

U.S.S.R., KAMCHATKA, Coastal Koryak. c. 1900
Photographer: Unknown. Donor: Miss Czaplicka

The Koryak are an arctic people related to the Asiatic Eskimo. Until recently the Coastal Koryak were dependent on hunting (particularly seal), fishing and gathering, supplemented by fur trading and reindeer breeding.

Koryak reindeer are semi-wild and are not broken to draw sledges as in other arctic cultures. This work is done by teams of dogs, which have to be strictly controlled to prevent them from attacking the reindeer. This photograph shows an extravagant sacrifice of almost a whole team of dogs which is made in the early spring to ensure the success of the new hunting season.

In the background is a semi-dugout house, the Coastal Koryak winter dwelling. Housing two or three related families, it is built on a pit reinforced with vertical logs rising to form an octagonal roof. The roof has a large funnel-shaped opening in the centre, as seen here. This is supported by poles. The opening serves as a smoke vent, window and winter entrance, the funnel shape protecting it from the effects of drifting snow.

The Coastal Koryak are now settled in fishing collectives.

JAPAN, YEZO, Ainu. c. 1865–1870
Photographer: Dammann Studio. Purchased 1901

The Ainu were the original inhabitants of the Japanese and southeast Soviet islands. Generally taller than the Japanese, the Ainu have thick beards and are often covered with hair. As in Siberian cultures, their economy and religious beliefs are based on hunting. In their sub-arctic climate they hunt bears, foxes, deer and salmon with spears, bows and poisoned arrows, traps and, latterly, guns.

The Ainu believe that good and evil spirits pervade every aspect of life and inhabit every object and animal. To placate these spirits and enlist their aid in hunting, willow wands with shaved bark streamers are placed as offering sticks in sacred places such as the eastern ends of houses. Bears, owls and eagles are killed ritually to 'send their spirits home' to the country where they assume their natural forms, which are human.

Their long tunics (*attush*) are made from the inner bark of elm trees, which is soaked and softened, separated into fibres and woven. Women often embroider garments with patterns peculiar to each village. Skin shoes and skin cloaks are worn in winter.

JAPAN. c. 1865–1870
Photographer: Dammann Studio. Purchased 1901

This street scene shows the favourite transport being used. The two-wheeled wooden carriage (*jinrikisha*) is pulled by a man who probably inherited the profession from his father. He wears functional clothing – a simple loincloth, dark blue sleeveless shirt, strong straw sandals and a headband – even in cold weather. These coolies have a reputation for endurance, speed and good humour as they trot along at about five miles per hour on the rough roads. Their qualities become invaluable during the frequent city traffic jams.

A popular song says, '*Jinrikisha* is so slow, drags along so wearily, bruises one's limbs and crushes when it overturns.'

Two café attendants bring the traveller a cup of rice wine (*saké*) on a tray. All wear the traditional rough silk or linen belted *kimono* and dress their hair into elaborate topknots. Their faces are whitened with flour powder. The girl travelling without a chaperone in the company of a man, however menial, exhibits more modern behaviour than usual for this time. It is probable that this scene is posed for the photographer.

CHINA. c. 1900
Photographer: Unknown. Donor: G. U. Price. 1905

A Buddhist nun in meditation holding a 'rosary' of 108 prayer beads. Buddhism was introduced into China in the Han dynasty (c. 202 B.C.–A.D. 220). Many thousands of monasteries and nunneries were founded where men and women lived according to Buddha's commandments for the preservation of human purity to assist man's progress in excellence and virtue.

Buddha himself is said to have permitted the establishment of nunneries so that his aunt and nurse could assume the Holy Life. However the appearance of nunneries is now thought to be much later. Buddhism never supplanted Confucianism as the religion of the State in China. It was subjected to centuries of spasmodic persecution and suffered from internal corruption. Nuns were always few in number and despised; by the time this photograph was taken they were no longer cloistered but forced to live in the houses of the laity. The final official demise of Buddhism was at the establishment of the People's Republic in 1949.

NEPAL, Newar. c. 1900
Photographer: Unknown. Donor: Dept. of Human Anatomy, Oxford, 1939

The Newar are farmers, craftsmen and small traders living mainly in the Kathmandu Valley. This photograph of women weaving was very probably posed to display various items of Newar textile technology.

The women are of the *Jyapoo* or farming class. They are recognisable by their distinctive dress; black sari edged with red, cotton blouse and huge waistbands. These clothes are made of home-produced cloth woven on looms such as this. The woman seated on the ground is demonstrating a spinning 'wheel' typical of the area. She turns the 'wheel' by a handle with her right hand, drawing out the thread on to a spool with the other. Nearby is a 'swift' on to which hanks of spun thread are wound; it is conical shaped to prevent the hank from dropping off the bottom.

Weaving is the main occupation for *Jyapoo* women after working in the family fields. Its importance is reflected in a Newar ceremony in which a bride's parents give her a spinning 'wheel' as part of her dowry. This tradition still survives even among high class urban Newar.

INDIA, MADHYA PRADESH. c. 1900
Photographer: Unknown. Donor: Dept. of Human Anatomy, Oxford, 1939

A sweetmeat seller at a market near Jabalpur. His goods are displayed on a metal tray and dishes, probably made of brass, which are supported by a wicker or canework stand. He is weighing out merchandise on a simple balance.

Only large towns have permanent bazaars. Villages hold weekly markets (*hāts*) and occasional fairs which are often associated with a religious festival. People and traders come in from the surrounding countryside to buy and sell and to exchange news and ideas. The traders usually work a circuit of markets in a locality. A wide range of goods is offered – shoes, pans, ornaments, vegetables, cloth, spices and so on. Sometimes fowl or goats are sold as well, although livestock is usually sold at a separate market. The price for a given commodity is not fixed but is subject to bargaining.

This economic network still functions. Modern developments have, if anything, strengthened it as improved communications make it easier for traders to move around a region.

SRI LANKA, Vedda. c. 1890
Photographer: Scowen & Co. Donor: E. B. Tylor

The Vedda have a very simple technology, living in caves and relying on hunting and gathering. They dismiss with contempt the belief, commonly held by the Sinhalese, that they were once rich and powerful; there does seem to be little evidence for it.

Every male Vedda carries a bow, feathered arrows and axe, as in this photograph. The bow is made of a sapling, shaved until the required flexibility is obtained, and a bark fibre string. The same fibre is used to bind arrow and axe heads to their shafts, the joint being sealed with resin. The iron arrow and axe heads are obtained by barter. The men here are wearing traditional Vedda garb of cotton or bark cloth wrapped round the body and between the legs. Each end is tucked into a waist string to keep it in place.

Today the Vedda of Sri Lanka have been almost totally absorbed into the modern Sinhalese population of the island.

ASSAM, NAGA HILLS, Ao Naga tribe. c. 1876
Photographer: Unknown. Donor: Lady Buckingham, 1932

A rare glimpse of the earliest missionaries to the Ao Nagas in the field: Rev. Dr. and Mrs. W. Clark of the American Baptist Missionary Society with porters and carrying chair. Dr. Clark arrived in the hill village of Molungyimchen in the spring of 1876. The Naga Hill tribes had a reputation for ferocity and head-hunting. It required considerable courage on the part of Dr. Clark to venture into the hills, outside the protection of the Colonial Government. However he did not reach the interior until after the pacification of the Ao Naga in 1894.

Conversion, despite every good intention, had serious effects on Ao Naga social and economic structure: for example, complete splits in villages, non-cooperation over essential agricultural work and non-participation in village politics.

BURMA. c. 1888
Photographer unknown. Donor: Miss M. Eyre; 1949

This photograph records the coming-of-age of the girl in the centre. On a day decreed as 'lucky' by an astrologer, girls of around eleven have their ears pierced with gold or silver needles by a professional ear-borer. Then he inserts permanent cylindrical studs, often of amber. After the ceremony the family holds a feast and gifts are given, as seen arrayed on the carpet here. The girl wears a court costume of embroidered Chinese silk which originated in a folk tale: a Burmese king out hunting came upon a bird maiden bathing; enchanted by her beauty, especially her marbled upturned tail feathers, he decreed that this plumage be reflected in women's court jackets. All women enhance their beauty by putting scented white flower powder on their faces.

The girl's brothers sit beside her. Ceremonials and feasting will also mark their attainment of adulthood. At about twelve, their legs will be tattooed and they will enter a Buddhist monastery for a period of education and initiation into the religion.

ANDAMAN ISLANDS. 1872
Photographer: G. E. Dobson. Donor: E. H. Man

On 4th May 1872 Dobson, a zoologist, went on a trip to visit an 'Andamanese Home' near Port Blair. Although the Andamanese were traditionally a non-sedentary hunting and gathering people, these settlements were set up by the authorities in order to foster friendly relations following the establishment of the Port Blair Penal Colony in 1858 after the Indian Mutiny.

On his visit Dobson took a series of excellent photographs, his only anthropological work. This one is full of interest. The two women in the foreground are wearing the finger and toe bones of their ancestors as necklaces. This practice was believed to guard against sickness. In the centre a widow wears the skull of her late husband on her shoulder. All wear rope girdles which are used for carrying small objects such as knives. The women also wear belts of pandanus leaf (bôd-da). The striking body decoration is renewed almost daily. Clay (odu) is mixed with water and applied to the body with fingers or, as here, the whole body is daubed and the pattern scraped away using a fish bone or bamboo splinter. Such decoration is common to both sexes.

NICOBAR ISLANDS, MALACCA. 1892
Photographer: E. H. Man. Donor: E. H. Man

E. H. Man, a government official, took this photograph just after the cyclone of March 1892 which caused considerable damage, particularly to the forest. The distinctive beehive roofed houses of the village are typical of the Nicobars although smaller rectangular structures are also built sometimes. They appear to have survived the storm well. They are strongly constructed, raised five to eight feet above the ground on piles driven well into the earth. The floor beams are secured across the piles by wooden pegs. The roof structure is then erected on the ground. Branches are lashed together with split cane to form the beehive shape. The framework completed, the assistance of all the men is summoned to lift the roof into position. They are rewarded with a feast of pork. Grass thatch, floor covering and walls are then added. The whole process is governed by supernatural considerations, for example, the door is never placed facing east for fear of evil spirits entering the house.

SARAWAK, BARAM RIVER, Kayan tribe. c. 1895
Photographer: C. Hose. Donor: Mrs. R. Shelford, 1975

Kayan villages normally comprise one long house built close to a river. Long houses are constructed of huge ironwood (*bilian*) piles with a ridge roof. They are often about 200 yards long, although many are even longer, and between 30 and 60 feet wide. They house about forty to sixty families. The floor is some 15 feet above ground level. Approximately half the width is divided off and partitioned into a private room for each family. The remainder forms an open gallery running the whole length of the house facing the river.

The gallery is, in effect, the village street where meetings are held and gossip exchanged. It also accommodates items in common use. Here are fish traps (the conical objects on the left) and a long narrow drum. In the middle distance are brass gongs (*tawak*) which are used in various ceremonies. These gongs are also used as currency. Opposite is a raised sleeping platform for bachelors and male visitors. To the right hang head trophies taken in war which are used in funerary rites.

SARAWAK, Iban (Sea Dayak). c. 1895
Photographer: C. Hose. Donor: Mrs. R. Shelford, 1975

A young man in all his finery. Iban men take great delight in their appearance; the standard item of clothing throughout Borneo and Sarawak is the waistcloth (*sirat*). Traditionally it was made of bark cloth but traded silk or cotton, as worn here, is much coveted. The quality and length (up to 15 yards) of the *sirat* are important displays of affluence. Here another piece of fine cloth is worn as a shawl (*dangdong*).

Excepting the elderly who are more restrained, the Iban wear magnificent ornaments, particularly earrings. The edge of the ear is pierced up to twenty times to carry an assortment of large brass rings and pendants. The bangles on the upper arm are of brilliant white *Kima* shell. Occasionally two are worn on each arm but this is considered bad taste. On the lower arm are *tumpa* bracelets, about sixty closely fitting rings, here probably made of ivory. The young man is carrying head-hunting trophies used in rituals. Other Sarawak tribes were also head-hunters but the Iban's aggressiveness and skill in war and head-hunting gave them a particular reputation for ferocity.

SOLOMON ISLANDS, SAN CRISTOVAL. 1873
Photographer: G. Smith for C. F. Wood. Donor: Mrs. Wood, 1921

One of a series of well documented photographs from Mr. C. F. Wood's cruise of the Pacific islands. It shows the canoe house at Makira. The canoe house is often the most important building in a village. Although simple in basic structure the decoration and furnishing is very lavish. The most striking feature is the central posts supporting the ridge pole; these are carved in human form with elaborate head dresses and ornament.

They house the treasured great war canoes which carry up to a hundred people. The canoes are elaborately decorated with high prow and stern, inlaid with white shell and hung with red tassels and strings of cowrie shells. Some of this detail can just be seen here. Canoe houses are also communal centres where men congregate, strangers are entertained and feasts held. The huge wooden bowls used for feast food are stored here. Jawbones of pigs eaten at feasts and skulls of enemies killed in war adorn the rafters.

NEW HEBRIDES (VANUATU), EFATE. c. 1885
Photographer: Capt. W. Acland. Donor: Capt. W. Acland, 1886

This photograph of a very fine group of upright slit gongs was taken during the cruise of H.M.S. *Miranda*. Slit gongs are of great importance in ancestor cults and in the rites of a graded society, a system by which men buy admittance to higher status and consequently greater social and political power by sacrificing pigs and giving feasts.

Gongs are stylised representations of ancestors erected individually by important men. They usually stand in a group beside a semi-sacred dancing ground. The manufacture of a gong involves complex rituals throughout. A large tree trunk, specially chosen, is hollowed out through the long vertical slit by experts and carved with an abstract 'face'. Whilst work is in progress the whole community is subject to special rules of behaviour. The gong is finally erected and put on general view amid much ritual feasting and sacrifice. It is also played at this stage. The lip of the slit is beaten with a stick and the gong sends out a deep booming sound. This represents the voice of the ancestor.

34

ELLICE ISLANDS (TUVALU), NUKUFETAU. 1873
Photographer: G. Smith for C. F. Wood. Donor: Mrs. Wood, 1921

Nukufetau is a small coral island in the Ellice group. The chief means of subsistence are fishing and gathering coconuts and other fruits. As on other Pacific islands coconut palm and pandanus (screw-pine) are in plentiful supply and provide the raw materials for most needs.

The dress of the girls in this photograph is a good example. They are wearing their dancing skirts, shell necklaces and flowers. The skirts are made of two or three layers of coconut palm leaf strips about half an inch wide which are knotted over a twisted coconut fibre cord. The strips on the outer layer are much finer than those underneath. Dancing skirts are decorated with a further layer of bunches of wide pandanus leaf streamers and feathers, coloured red, black and yellow. They are worn over padded belts of palm leaf to make them stand out. Skirts for daily use do not have decorations and, being subjected to heavy wear, have to be replaced regularly.

GILBERT ISLANDS (KIRIBATI). c. 1890
Photographer: G. Balfour. Donor: G. Balfour, 1897

The Gilbert Islands are a group of sixteen small coral islands in Micronesia. Settlements are scattered along the edges of lagoons and are usually inhabited by extended family groups. Although individual settlements are isolated, they are interdependent and share a central meeting house often near the chief's dwelling.

This photograph shows the interior of the meeting house (*maneaba*). It is possible that this particular one at Maraki was not in regular use when photographed as the roof seems to be in a state of disrepair. It is none the less an impressive structure. The gabled roof rises on the outside from short coral limestone pillars set into the ground, and is supported by poles made of coconut palm trunks. The roof principals are also made of large coconut palm beams with secondary rafters of pandanus. The thatch is of pandanus leaf attached to coconut wood battens.

The men gather in the *maneaba* to discuss business and exchange gossip. They sit on floor mats, each man having an ancestral place, the traditional seat of his kin. The *maneaba* is also used for entertaining visitors, ceremonies and feasting.

NEW ZEALAND, MAORI. c. 1900.
Photographer: J. Martin. Donor: H. Balfour

The Maori are a Polynesian people who colonised New Zealand long before Europeans arrived. They have a complex social, religious and material culture and are known for their elaborate carvings with curvilinear designs. Such patterns can be seen tattooed on this man's face and carved on his staff-club. Tattooing, done with a sharp bone tool and a pine-ash pigment rubbed into the cut, marks a man as a tribal chief. Here, Mohi Te Pongamau carries a chief's wooden staff-club (*taiaha*), which is decorated with hair from the now extinct Maori white dog and parrot feathers. The club's carving suggests a face with a protruding tongue – an expression used by Maori warriors to frighten enemies before attacking.

He wears a dress cape of twined flax with rolled yellow flax leaf streamers. These serve the dual purpose of shedding water and rustling when shaken, announcing the chief's presence. His ear pendant (*kuru*) is greenstone, similar to jade.

AUSTRALIA, NEW SOUTH WALES, CLARENCE RIVER. c. early 1870's
Photographer: J. W. Lindt. Lent by Miss Hands, 1934

This posed studio portrait shows the aborigine Louis and his wife 'in the wild'. The photographer is obviously trying to exhibit as much of their material culture as possible, and so includes some anomalies. Native men do hunt kangaroo, wallaby, emu and other game with wood- or stone-pointed spears and boomerangs, but women usually collect roots and grubs – they do not hunt, as suggested here. Aborigines usually do not hunt or eat the animal which shares their tribal ancestor and thus becomes their 'totem'. The ancestors of humans and animals are believed to have been mythical beings who roamed the land during 'the Dreamtime'. Their journeys and deeds are commemorated in rituals; the men dance, chant myths and bring out sacred objects usually kept hidden.

Men do not wear skin aprons as shown here, although they may use skin cloaks for warmth. The vegetable fibre bag hanging from the branch is commonly used for the transport of possessions when small family groups travel in search of food and water.

38

TASMANIA, TRUGANINA. 1866
Photographer: probably C. Woolley. Prints by Beattie, Hobart. Purchased 1895

The original inhabitants of Tasmania were probably related to the natives of Australia. Their culture was the simplest to have survived into recent times, being based mainly on hunting game with wooden spears and collecting shellfish, wild fowl eggs and wild vegetable foods. Early European contacts remarked upon the gentleness, simplicity and contentedness of the natives. However, British settlers regarded them as hostile and they were driven from their territory, hunted and decimated by disease. The surviving aborigines were confined to a settlement on Flinders Island in the north, where they could not pursue their traditional means of subsistence since little game or fresh water existed.

When the British arrived in 1804, the population was estimated to be 5000. At the time of this group photograph only fourteen were left living, at Oyster Cove near Hobart. Truganina, once married to the chief of the Bruni Island tribe, died in 1876 – the last full-blooded native Tasmanian.

TASMANIA, OYSTER COVE. 24th March 1858
Photographer: probably Bishop Nixon. Purchased 1895

BIBLIOGRAPHY

General texts on anthropology and material culture.

Barnett H. G.	*Innovation. The Basis of Cultural Change.* 1953.
Beattie J.	*Other Cultures.* 1966.
Coon C.	*The Hunting People.* 1976.
Firth R.	*Human Types.* rev. ed. 1975.
Forde C. D.	*Habitat, Economy and Society.* 1934.
Johnson D. L.	*The Nature of Nomadism.* 1969.
Lévi-Strauss C.	*Tristes Tropiques.* trans. 1973.
Lewis I. M.	*Social Anthropology in Perspective.* 1976.
Mair L.	*An Introduction to Social Anthropology.* 2nd. ed. 1972.
—	*Observers of Man.* 1980. Catalogue of an exhibition of photographs from the Royal Anthropological Institute.
Richardson M. ed.	*The Human Mirror.* 1974.
Service E. R.	*Profiles in Ethnology* 3rd ed. 1978.
Spier R. F. G.	*From the Hand of Man.* 1970.

The following titles are more detailed ethnographies of some of the peoples covered in this volume. However, a number of them are old and may be difficult to find.

Batchelor J.	*The Ainu of Japan.* 1892.
Bridges E. L.	*The Uttermost Part of the Earth.* 1948.
Buck P.	*The Coming of the Maori.* 2nd ed. 1952.
Codrington R.	*The Melanesians.* 1891.
Collinder B.	*The Lapps.* 1949.
Cranstone B. A. L.	*The Australian Aborigines.* 1973.
Drucker P.	*Indians of the Northwest Coast.* 1955.
Hose C. & McDougall W.	*The Pagan Tribes of Borneo.* 1912.
Koch G.	*Die Materielle Kultur der Ellice-Inseln.* 1961.
Koch G.	*Materielle Kultur der Gilbert-Inseln.* 1965.
Krige E. J.	*The Social System of the Zulu.* 1936.
Layard J.	*Stone Men of Malekula.* 1942.
Levin M. G. & Potapov L. P.	*The Peoples of Siberia.* trans. 1964.
Lowie R. H.	*The Crow Indians.* 1935.

Man E. H.	*The Nicobar Islands and Their People.* 1931.
Mills J. P.	*The Ao Naga.* 1926.
Nepali G. S.	*The Newars.* 1965.
Radcliffe-Brown A. R.	*The Andaman Islands.* 1964. repr.
Roth H. L.	*The Aborigines of Tasmania.* 2nd ed. 1899.
Seligmann C. G. & B. Z.	*The Veddas.* 1911.
Turner G.	*Indians of North America.* 1979.
Vuorela T.	*The Finno-Ugric Peoples.* 1964.

A Lapp girl and her dog. c. 1890's. Photographer: Unknown

ACKNOWLEDGEMENTS

We are very grateful to the following people from the Pitt Rivers Museum staff for their help and advice: Mr. R. Inskeep, Dr. S. Jones, Dr. H. La Rue, Mr. R. Rivers, Dr. D. Tayler, Mr. J. Todd, and in particular Miss F. J. Cousins, Mr. B. A. L. Cranstone and Mr. V. P. Narracott. We would also like to thank Mr. F. Cameron, Miss C. Cech, Dr. O. Impey, Mr. M. McLeod, Mrs. R. Poignant, Mr. R. Summers, and Mr. G. Turner.

Back cover:
U.S.A., NEW MEXICO, RIO GRANDE. 1879
Photographer: J. K. Hillers. Donor: E. B. Tylor

The Governor of San Juan Pueblo. Chosen by the priest fraternities, the Governor takes charge of everyday tribal matters. Any man who serves the community in a religious or secular way becomes one of the 'Made People', a true spiritual man of the tribe. In their words, 'Within and around the earth, within and around the mesas, within and around the mountains, your authority returns to you one time, two times, three times, four times.'